THE POEMS OF B.R. WHITING

ALSO BY B.R. WHITING

The Little Desert: Poems of India, Australia and Italy (1978)
Winter for Quiet: A Collection of Sea Poems (1979)

The Poems of B.R. Whiting

The Sheep Meadow Press
Riverdale-on-Hudson, New York

All inquiries and permission requests should be addressed to: The Sheep Meadow Press, P.O. Box 1345, Riverdale-on-Hudson, New York 10471.

Distributed by I.L.P.A.
P.O. Box 816
Oak Park, IL 60303

Typesetting by Keystrokes, Lenox, Massachusetts
The book was composed in Mergenthaler Bembo
Printed by Princeton University Press

Library of Congress Cataloging-in-Publication Data
Whiting, B. R. (Bertrand R.), 1923–1989
[Poems. Selections]
The poems of B.R. Whiting.
p. cm.
ISBN 1-878818-08-2
I. Title.
PR9619.3.W518A6 1991
821—dc20 91-11885
CIP

CONTENTS

A Remembrance of B.R. Whiting by Stanley Moss

The Little Desert and Uncollected Poems

Introduction to *The Little Desert* (1978)—Christopher Fry 3

SECTION ONE

Gandhi, 1946 7
Smell of Man 8
Our Sad Monarchies 10
Summer Palace, Darjeeling 11
Ceremony 12
Splitting Firewood 13
Tiger Shooting in Bengal 14
I, the Elder 15
Silence 16

SECTION TWO

Renewing the Queen 19
Vermin Hunt 21
Hoplite 22
Smile Please 23
Foreshadowed 26
And the Dark Falling 27
For Sale: Robe, South Australia 28

Winter for Quiet and Uncollected Poems

The Feel of the Sea 31
Choice 32
Sailing on Lago di Vico 33
Cervinia 34

Historical Research 35
Philosophy 36
The White Stoat 37
Operation of Memory 38
"Servyn", 4/5/78 39
Picture 40
A Low Profile 41
Judgement 42
Signal 43
Giant Swing 44
To Get Ready for a Journey 45
The Coast 46
The Gaoler 48
To Impose a Sea Change 49
What Grotesque Version 50
Gone Away 51
Wake 52
Whales 53
After 54
Limits of Knowledge 55
Sunken Church, Cittaducale 56
The Circle Closes 57
Hadrian's Villa 58
Dancing 59
Heard, Shared and Remembered 60
Blind Chess 61
Focus 62
The Facts 63
Sense 64
In the Telescope of the Sextant 66
Les Moines 67
Navigation 68
The First Morning 69
Inland at Last 71
The Visitors 72
The Optimists 73
By the Plough 74

Gone 75
Summer Calm 76
Still Night 77
Haunted by the Sea 78
In Kit Form 79
Stretto di Piombino 80
Winter in Town 81
St. Florent, Corsica 82
Conquest 83
The Wanderer 84
You Go He 85
Winter for Quiet 86
Holiday 87
But— 89
Knowledge 90
Mooring Flowers 91
Cruising in Autumn 92

Afterword—Carolyn Kizer 93

Whiting in Venice, 1977

A REMEMBRANCE OF B.R. WHITING

We met by mistake—his first evening in Rome, September, 1955—he had gone to a reception to meet an old friend, Major W. Stanley Moss, parachuting hero of the Battle of Crete. He got me instead. B.R. Whiting was the last of the courtier-soldier poets. Born the second of three brothers to a landed Australian family, he lied about his age, enlisted in the Australian army in 1939, and fought through the terrible New Guinea campaign. After that defeat, he joined the British Army in India, where he became Aide-de-Camp to the Governor of Bengal, an Australian friend of his family, Lord-to-be, R.G. Casey. He served till the end of the Raj. Decorated, witty, and handsome, but for one punch in the finals, the middleweight champion of the Australian Army, young Captain Whiting flourished in the presence of Casey, Lord Mountbatten, and Mahatma Gandhi. Fearing Gandhi would be assassinated, Whiting urged Casey and Gandhi to let him be Gandhi's bodyguard. But Gandhi refused.

Thirteen years later, in 1959 in Rome, Whiting began writing poetry in secret. His first poem, "Gandhi, 1946," preserves a moment of personal spiritual revelation, the memory of Gandhi's hand resting on Whiting's arm and what touching that arm meant to an Indian servant. Such moments are found throughout this book; they may well be what the book is about.

In the Twentieth Century, no poet writing in English, out of uniform after the wars, continued to think of himself as a soldier—certainly not Robert Graves, Randall Jarrell, James Dickey, or even the mug Roy Campbell in his tin can armor laboring as a picadore in Spain. The Bertie Whiting I knew thought of himself as a soldier in his life and in his poetry:

HOPLITE

The voice said, Jeez I love to punch a Pom!

I looked, he was Australian, young and brown,
A cyclist with a fighting face, and from
His story, he had knocked the bastards down
On street and stairway when he had excuse
More for their fat, their whining city days
Their little views for which he had no use
Than for a fault. Nature adores the ways
Of war, and though I looked at him in hate
I felt the furnace where his blood was fired,
Conscious my wit could never compensate
For the iron muscles, and my heart admired
The hoplite, the phalanx that never tires,
The cruel eye for loot, the cropped crown,
The beautiful body that props up the Empires
And brings them crashing down.

After India gained independence, Whiting returned to Australia. Both parents had died—his father had wassailed away a fortune and left a Himalayan mountan of debt. Whiting did his best to pay those debts. University study among the young and inexperienced had become impossible. Whiting went instead into the Australian bush, into The Little Desert and The Ninety-Mile Desert, with a sack of books, among the other kangaroos, to work as a traveling bee-keeper.

He had spent most of his boyhood at school in the countryside with a horse under him, often jumping without reins. The desert and bush, reading and bee-keeping, no doubt offered more truth, peace, and fun than the sillier hives of Melbourne society. He knew more about nature than most poets I have known. As other poets might get their hands into the soil of a garden, he went into the desert, up the Matterhorn, schussed across alpine ravines, sailed on and into dangerous seas. He grabbed at nature that was too wild to hold. "Nature adores the ways/Of war," he wrote. And so did he, but he was too spiritual for that alone.

In 1948, he married the sculptor and painter, the well-to-do Lorri Fraser, a love from childhood. They lived a couple of years in Australia, mostly in the country. They kept bees, he wrote a column called "A Country Diary" for a Melbourne newspaper. He read mostly history, fiction, and English poetry. He published a few comic short stories. Whiting would eventually teach himself decent French, German, Spanish, Greek, and, of course, Italian. They migrated to the English countryside, stayed for two years, followed by a year in London, before going to Rome in 1955, where he spent most of the next thirty years he had to live. He would return to Australia, in all those years, only several times amounting to a matter of weeks, although Lorri Fraser's brother, Malcolm Fraser, became Prime Minister.

In his own sweet way, Whiting spent his life walking English Bulldogs in Old Rome, laughing, talking, reading, drinking, his soul at risk, writing poetry, loving, sailing and skiing (any order I might choose would be untrue). They did what they wanted to do, yet it seemed to me they did not do what they wanted to do: he lived a life of self-imposed tragical-comical exile, but it was exile nonetheless. He did not long for an Australian Jerusalem, nor was it simply that he was a fish out of water, but that his deepest yearnings were elsewhere. It is not by chance that most of his poems are concerned with his early days in India and Australia, others are set in the No-Man's-Land of alpine snows, or at sea. Every word, every line he wrote, was Australian, filled with Down Under cadence and pitch, an unruly prisoner of its English origins.

Sometimes, when reading someone else's poems to friends, he would burst into tears. I remember his weeping when he read aloud Auden's poem, "The Shield of Achilles." I remember my being bewildered when he wept. Now, it seems to me he could not help remembering his dead. It was two years before he wrote his first poem.

In those early days beside the Tiber, I questioned him endlessly about the Australian deserts, the codes of dogs, tigers, bees, horses, butterflies, and the motherliness of kangaroos, about which he seemed to know everything. He knew, more than anyone I was ever in a position to question, about India, Gandhi, Asian poverty, British, Sikkh and Japanese soldiers, the Etruscans, the Aborigines of New Guinea and Australia, the world's untouchables. He had a soldier's loyalty to friends and a soldier's admiration for courage and physical strength in people and in animals. He knew the exact number of pounds of pressure an English Bulldog's jaws could put upon a board. He had a special eye for the courage and durability of any living thing, not excluding trees, the Mediterranean, and certain mountains. The Bertie Whiting I knew was the kindliest, the sweetest and gentlest of men. He could not for long be separated from his smile and laughter. He was a virtuoso of jest, a gift beyond the mere good sense of humor given to others. His seriousness was occasionally accompanied by a mortal trumpet call of military bluster that, to me, served the cause of merriment. Still, it was human frailty, his own and others', that broke his heart.

Very few years ago, after Prime Minister Aldo Moro was assassinated, he told me, and he was serious, that he was thinking of offering himself as a bodyguard to dignitaries whose lives and kneecaps had been threatened by the Red Guard. I put him at table with a wild group of soldier-poets: Sydney and Raleigh, Mao Tse-Tung, the young Edgar Allen Poe at West Point, and Yehuda Amichai.

This book is, of course, without a dedication, but there is no doubt that it is into Lorri's hands that he would have rendered it. On his death in 1989 he left behind two chapbooks, piles of poems, and many scrawled pages of manuscript. Christopher Fry and I went over everything separately and then together on two occasions. Nothing either of us thought should be in this book was excluded. It is possible further work could produce new discoveries. The arrangement was my choice. Nothing in our friendship, except his death, brought anything but joy to my heart.

Stanley Moss

The Little Desert
and Uncollected Poems

Introduction to *The Little Desert* (1978)

Rome: Spring or early Summer, 1958. The playwright and novelist Bridget Boland took my wife and me to visit her Australian friends B.R. Whiting and his wife, the abstract painter Lorri, in their flat beside the Tiber. It was the start of a now twenty-year-old friendship, of Italian evenings whenever I was in Rome film-writing, of English days whenever they came over for Lorri's exhibitions of painting in Davies Street or at the I.C.A., or on visits to our Sussex home. But though I had known from Bridget that Bertie was often busy writing he never talked about what he was doing, and after our first meeting several years went by before I was let in to at least part of the secret, and that only came about through Lorri. I had gone to their flat for dinner—by this time they had moved deeper into Trastevere—and Lorri had put on the little table beside my chair a sheet of paper bearing a few typewritten lines. It was the poem *Gandhi, 1946.* Nothing was said, but I picked it up and read it. My delight in the poem broke through Bertie's reticence, and other poems came my way: the vivid recall of life in Australia, where for a time they kept bees, from which, as well as honey, came the fascinating poem *Renewing the Queen;* of India, where Bertie was Aide-de-Camp to Mr. R.G. Casey just after the War; and of Italy, of skiing at Cervinia, of sailing on Lago di Vico or in wilder waters. The difficulty has been to decide which poems, out of such a range, should be included in this selection; some were in close contention, others—*Vermin Hunt,* for instance, and the lovely *And The Dark Falling,* simply chose themselves.

Christopher Fry

With Lorri, in Rome 1955

SECTION ONE

GANDHI, 1946

Did you like him? No. What was it, then?
He had a memorable laugh.
Did you like his disciples? No, not at all,
They had the vestry air.
Yet you remember him? Oh yes, unforgotten
The bright eye and the paper light
Hand on my arm when I walked with him.

Only that? No, time has eaten away
The resentment at a power
That presumed on my arm for its strength,
And now I like to think
How, after I had escorted him to the car,
The Khitmugar came up
To ask permission, if he might touch that arm.

SMELL OF MAN

On a Temple in dim light
Being more than they seem
Hindu figures writhe
Binding life and its stirring
To the odorless stone.

The hierarchy of night
Fruit-eaters flap the upper air
Black bats flutter retreat
Hang as daylight insects come.

Cattle couched at ease, eyes glow,
No fowl scratches the graveyard gate
But a solitary, military cock crows.

A tram rocks alive along the street
The driver dazed with heat.

Ganges slips a brown stain to the sea,
Grain-ships clank at their moorings.

Under the eaves rats big as cats,
Families in sweat and sleep
Their hell its own place
Breathing the close smell of man.
Over Calcutta the kites wheel and turn,
Vultures belch.

Holy Sadhu
Revolves in the filth of cities,
Stirs in his dream,
Things are as they are,
More than they seem:

The raptors and a tall dog
See the movement, stealthily
Control the moment—his smell
Warns them of his deadly health.

On a mound of refuse
Feebly under the weight of air
A dying child moves, abandoned,
The tall dog comes from the alley
Its purpose given to the kites
Who alert the vultures.

The doors are shut.

On the yellow walls, dung cakes
For the small fires of morning
For the smell of man, drying,
A hand imprinted in dung.

OUR SAD MONARCHIES

Is there a structure that stands up to time
That whistles in the wind when we're away
With the same tune? Do details hold their line,
Do the proportions stay?
We have added ourselves to make reality,
The selves we add being dreams and being there;
Without the dream, things lose their credibility
In quite another order:
These familiar limbs,
The closest animal,
Turn into tombs,
Merge in the real—
Grown out of chaos to kill us, the linked teams
Of atoms have their iron priorities,
To claim the bodies and ignore the dreams,
Smoke from the pyre of our sad monarchies.

SUMMER PALACE, DARJEELING

FROM the terrace, shivering miles
Of valleys, hills and rivers
To the grave snowfields of Kanchenjunga;

From the terrace a fall
Over the precipice into streamers
Of mist rising from Bengal and Bhutan;

In the garden bulbuls call
The lament for warriors,
Water spills tuneful, serenading,

And typical flowers fill
Evenings with english hours
While ghurka sentries are parading.

In the garden it is possible
To remember the powers
Of Moghul, Viceroy, Genghis Khan

And envy the tales
Of days more colourful than ours
And the verses the horsemen sang—

The helmet crumples,
The good lance shivers,
The tent of the great Khan stands alone—

From the terrace the calls
Of a charcoal seller
Shiver the peace and the splendour is gone

Because he paid for it all,
The small, condemned loser,
Who is shut out of the hilltop garden.

CEREMONY

To watch the sun rise on the Himalayas
We climbed into Nepal with a guide
And found ourselves faced by an airless void,
A pale shroud ringed by pall-bearers:
There in the distance forms that we had known
Of men who would never return
Remembered in forbidding ceremony—
Gods in an amphitheatre, still, withdrawn,
Giants on a memorial, guards in white,
Mutes one by one in order of their height
Were capped by the bright flame of dawn:
Everest, Kanchenjunga, Makalu, names
Vibrating like slow bells for the fallen
As a new day for the world began
In Burma, China, Karakorum—
Burned out the hollow where the night was frozen
The Roll Call ended, and the brief flame;
And still we lingered by the tomb
Long after the sun had risen.

SPLITTING FIREWOOD

SPLITTING firewood I often found
Fat white grubs in the grain
And would toss them on the ground—
The fowls learned this, and a vain
Old crow who posed apart in liberty
Used to wait for me to throw
The juicy ones under his special tree,
Where he would stab them straight
Before the frantic fowls arrived—
Bird-brain, they were in such a state,
The brown contentious crowd that lived
In a clucking strain of imitation.
But then, a cackling hen, meanly
By cunning, running to look
Would try to beat the mob to it again,
Push up, put her head on the block,
Staring, arrogant, stupid, plain,
And I would cut it off, throw
It to the black and elegant crow
Who did not rely on my offering—
There was no change in the fowlyard cries,
They were indifferent to headless suffering,
And he would peck out its opal eyes.

TIGER SHOOTING IN BENGAL

When I tell the story, I was really one,
As hard and eager in the Big-Game rite
As any other gun—but I alone
Hated to wait for tiger in the night;

Ancestral anger I could understand,
Share a tiger's hunger, that's quite fair,
But not the level stare and the steady hand
Nerveless in the shivering jungle air:

I could see through the hot gold eye of the cat,
Feel for the tethered goat on the ground,
I might have saved them both, and yet
I gave no warning, made no sound—

The hard edge of truth, then,
Insists I was keen,
Anxious to have been
Liked by those sporting men.

I, THE ELDER

—once I stood
In a dawn on the Torsa River near Nilpara,
The quiet mahogany forest pale with rain,
Looking at half a brindle cow, torn
By a tigress and her cubs, their tracks clear.
We were unarmed; Sen. Gupta waved his hand,
Pointed, and the man-tall ranks of grass
Bent in the early breeze and split apart
To show them lying there: they made no sound
But slowly turned, their coats glowing,
And the tigress stared back with the eyes
Both shy and proud, of Susannah bathing.

SILENCE

Your first parachute jump, after the waterfall of sound:
What surprises is to hang in silence—but you are not still,
There is a flutter of silk, the earth bulges up all round
And with a resounding thump you return to normal;
And in the desert at noontide
When the insects pause and the baking claypan cracks
There is still the regular surf of your blood
On the reef of your ears, echoing back;
They say it is true the stars sing in their freedom,
The atoms raise an inaudible hymn and rejoice,
We are attuned to noises, not to the vacuum:
In silence we hear the still, small voice.
Unlike lust and self-sacrifice, loyalty and treason,
The idea of silence has a false quality,
A fiction deriving from our fault
Like the immaculate, like immortality.

SECTION TWO

RENEWING THE QUEEN

PALE in the shadow of a Springtime fable
The death-cup fungus white as candle wax,
The wild orchids have become invisible
Under knotted flowers and grass and sticks,
Volcanic stones as round as rotting skulls
Fade into the ground, live in other lives,
The bird droppings are imperial purple;
It is time to open the marked beehives.

The signs of age are clearly there to see,
An early shrinkage in the brood chamber,
Dark drones round the door, worn soldiery,
Too few workers and not of pure colour,
A tone of doubt in the way the hive sings,
An angry outcry when it is open,
A smell of decay, these are the things
That help us decide to kill the Queen.

She runs on the centre comb, betrayed
By the attention of her guardians—
A hand swoops to pinch off her head
And drops her body inside again;
Throughout the hours the news is spread
Of a communal death in a panic rage
Until we come to replace the dead
With an amber Queen in a wooden cage.

Escorted by courtiers due to die,
Caught behind a wall of sugar,
A stranger among her enemies—
To kill her they must devour the door,

But as they eat their sure way in
Fight her knights through hours of malice
Her unknown odour becomes their own,
They swarm to murder and stay to kiss,

Fawn on the shower sent down from God,
Dance in the sun, show their ways content,
A work-song raised to say that it is good,
Rebirth praised in an ordered monument.
We share the vital nature of their gain,
The deep vibrations of their harmony,
A sacred activity, if one remains,
And the reward is more than honey.

VERMIN HUNT

TAKE a piece of metal, say
The top of a bootpolish tin;
Pierce it the right way,
Bend it double in
Your mouth, and you can fake
The scream of agony trapped rabbits make.

One night I took this hunting sound
To the open plain where the land is dry,
And sat in sheepskins, flat down to the ground,
And shot the foxes as they stalked the cry.

Midnight was still, the Cross an icy light,
The sky black and dead in its slow parade,
And as I whistled, shrieked, a shade of night
Swooped on me, soundless, saw me, swayed
And banked, wide and dark on the wing—
An instant—but how my heart had prayed,
Fluttered, knowing itself a naked thing
Hunted by the horned owl, and afraid.

HOPLITE

THE voice said, Jeez I love to punch a Pom!

I looked, he was Australian, young and brown,
A cyclist with a fighting face, and from
His story, he had knocked the bastards down
On street and stairway when he had excuse
More for their fat, their whining city days
Their little views for which he had no use
Than for a fault. Nature adores the ways
Of war, and though I looked at him in hate
I felt the furnace where his blood was fired,
Conscious my wit could never compensate
For the iron muscles, and my heart admired
The hoplite, the phalanx that never tires,
The cruel eye for loot, the cropped crown,
The beautiful body that props up the Empires
And brings them crashing down.

SMILE PLEASE

YEARS ago, when I was in my prime,
Fit to uproot the trees, on a day's end
When the swallows shuttled swiftly home
And there was an evening hour to spend,

I took my rifle to the desert edge
Where scrub joins crop, and hesitated
What I should kill; by the pink heath
My mind was made up, and I waited.

Golden daylight wasted faintly
Into the finest horizontal grey,
Out of the native grass the Mallee parrot
Rose in a talking cloud and flew away,

Out of the salty swamp the emu stalked
Into the ti-tree thicket, and the late
Flight of the honey-eaters evaporated
Leaving the world hollow and desolate,

Arched by the spaces of an ancient sky
Where nothing that was young was ever born,
A fox barked, hardly a tree stirred,
Day died old, forsaken and forlorn.

They were betrayed by sunset's treachery,
The kangaroos, lit by the slanting light,
Approaching from the west, prickeared, alert,
Their one defence the spurt, the speed of flight.

Silence was air; only myself and they
Breathed on the earth; their gentle innocence
Challenged my blood, summoned me to my prey

Among the bushes growing to the fence
And drew my lips back—was it in a smile?

They grazed the open field in the light's ebb,
They gazed around for danger—mile on mile
Only the black thick border of the scrub
That sent out sentinels of single trees
Spaced here and there under the velvet air.

Lowering little hands down to the earth
They cropped the grain, and grinning with the bare
Chance of the moment, crouching up I came,
Waiting and watching not to move too soon,
Stalking, imitating their walking pace,
Tense and unblinking—and up came the moon.

Then they were blackened shapes that shot up heads
In knife-sharp outline, and I was a black,
Still, rounded bush, advanced into the crop—
Unstirring, steady: slowly they bent back.

When they were eating, I moved carefully,
If they looked up, I froze into the trees,
In the wild moonlit plain I came to them
Slow as the hours and silent as disease.

Beside me in the night I saw a doe
Delicately licking in her fur,
Twitching her nose, scratching her narrow chest,
Quite unaware of what was coming to her—

And while she calmly looked at me, I shot her.

(Notice they grind their jaws when dying, they
Curl little paws against the bloody fur,
The great legs stretch and kick the world away.)

In the wide plain, under the gaping moon,
Was only Death and the quivering carrion dead,
Her companions scattered swift as a flight of birds,
And in alarm I raised my startled head—

Wherever I calmly pursue my chosen path,
No matter how clear the way, how flat the plain,
If I watch myself I ought to be all right—
Whenever I relax it moves again—

It was allotted to me from the start—
It has the time and energy to spare—
Its shape is shadow and its hands are strong—
Its lips are drawn back, and the teeth are bare.

FORESHADOWED

Is the paean of wind in telephone wires
Still answered by the hush of man-tall thistles
And, in a dry land, the cry of seagulls
Driven by Southern storms to that crowsfoot clay,
Does the hawk fall away down air blown dry
To stoop over plover chicks frozen safe,
Does it flap heavily to a fence-post
Pursued by the same metallic screams,
Do the foxes bark in the black-frost night
With a lost complaint, and a claim,
Has the windmill's beat a broken lilt
As dawn wakes the plain, and the overspill
Imitates valleys of urgent green,

Or do these memories play on me, alone?
Do they stir a frozen mind as once the wind
Ruffled the down of a hare in her brittle sett,
Cramped, unable to run as the hounds came
And the horsemen, long foreshadowed, out of the rising sun?

AND THE DARK FALLING

IN the shade of a tree like a hand in the wind
Your pale straw hat the echo of the hay
Eyes grey to green, arms brown as the land,
Setting out scones, white mugs of tea—

Midsummer weather for the new hay baler
Light like malice grinning on fresh paint
And through the voice of the chanting tractor
A new-mown pasture's sweet food scent—

Tied with twine of an undergrowth green
The future itself, the bales on the stubble,
And over the fence the pointed horns
And deep red flanks of Hereford cattle—

We seemed immortal, side by side, riding
Home on the trailer, singing, calling,
Our backs turned to the horned moon sliding
Steadily to Autumn, and the dark falling.

FOR SALE: ROBE, SOUTH AUSTRALIA

Beside the road the cliffs are golden sandstone
Glowing, pitted, honeycombed by the wind,
And the wild bees thrive on the velvet heather
By the white star-clusters of the ti-tree;
In the salty swamp the Banksia is a giant,
Gnarled, yielding a rank, personal honey;
The approach forbidding, dark warden scrub,
And beyond the cliffs the sound of the working sea—
The garden gate locked for a generation
Has been plaited shut by a rhododendron;
You drive round to the back, among the sparrows
Chattering over the grain by the empty stable,
To a first sight of a once-white window frame,
A wall of the honeyed stone behind a vine,
And beneath the wheelbarrow a black snake
Immobile, swallowing a rat—
The dogs do not bark, and when you knock
They will not try to leave the verandah,
Feeling that time has seized the dying farm,
Hearing above your voice the bees in the cliff
And the rustle of the sand in the rank grass.

Winter for Quiet
and Uncollected Poems

THE FEEL OF THE SEA

THE Pacific was always cold: I preferred the sand;
The Americans on a visit started the rot;
My heart was seduced less by the guns and the band
Than by the elegance I could sense in the Fleet;
We never caught a sight of the water, not one,
But how could anyone doubt of the sea's glamour?
Nobody else had on what I had on,
A gob hat given me by a gigantic sailor.

The kiss of the cool air turning pink with the sun,
The smell from the shipyard of the salty wood,
The purity of a morning just begun
That is still enticing, stretching out ahead;
I can almost taste the calm,
Feel how heavy to pull she was, "The Jack,"
And no sound at all in that empty dawn
But the ripples of our passing, rowing back;
Beaching her, bailing her by the beam,
Counting the fish, feeling my stomach turn
For the taste and the kiss that never leave my lips,
On mornings we went out with the harpoon.

My earliest memory of the sea is of Neptune:
After sand-castles came the initiation;
Arms round his neck red with expensive lotion,
My Father towed me out; the afternoon
Was dedicated to him in some way,
Perhaps to recognise his condescension—
Off Philip Island, later, drenched in spray
I saw shoulders like that on a sea-lion.

CHOICE

MEMORY has no diamonds;
Precious stones, yes, beautiful,
But the ultimate cutting tool
Is the moment, good or bad:

It is for this jewel I choose to start
In rough weather, treasuring the thrill
When we cast off, set sail,
Fear once more kindled in the heart.

SAILING ON LAGO DI VICO

ONE hour from the city and alone on the water
Towering fine-weather clouds and a breeze from the West
One thousand five hundred feet above the coast
We are sailing on the heart of a lost Empire.

The sapphire surface is smooth and clean as a plate;
Few Romans come here, they believe in a whirlpool
Or the bad luck of lakes—within the crater walls
We feel safe in a hand that holds us up, as pets,

But the white hull and the taut sail of order
Are denied by the wake of the boat, immediately
Wiped out, like the Etruscans and their Navy—
Tracks made on water.

CERVINIA

To be on the slopes of the Matterhorn
Is to feel the bow-surge proud of Europe,
And the keen air inciting
To the downward swoop of the swallow,
The cloud-free rush and the wind-
Fast white descent of the skiers.

And to brave,
(comfortably sure of return)
The winter tempest and the muffling snow
Is to sense the power, the constant,
Inimical, indifferent strength
Of geological time, a planet-ship
Sailing past the command of any crew.

I envy the eagle, marmot, wolf of the Grandes Jurasses
And go with the turning globe,
And not against it—
I take warning from the cloud-raker
Goring the sky, crowned with sunset, growing—
And go with the Matterhorn, glad for a moment
To be part of that great bull head.

HISTORICAL RESEARCH

AFTER her funeral, and the newspapers,
And the Insurance were all cleared up,
The wreck of the Fiat sold for scrap
And life proceeding on its way,

I borrowed his tape-recorder for a day
To use in some historical research.
He had forgotten to erase the sound
And out of laughter came his voice
Teaching a parrot, a present for her,
Saying over and over,
Where's Rosamund?
        Say, Where's Rosamund?
                Where's Rosamund?
                        Say, Where's Rosamund?

PHILOSOPHY

I don't know much about reception,
Intellection, reality, meaning, wisdom—
I tried to learn all about perception
From a wise old man, still handsome—
He told me from his bed I should proceed
By stepping-stones of Plato and the fine
Arguments of Schoolmen—I should read
Gradually Russell, Wittgenstein,
Along with Aristotle. Now the years
Say merely he was kind, and I'm prepared
To read philosophy and calm my fears—
Yet nothing learned is half to be compared
To the deep refreshing sleep that healed my youth
After about ten pages of the Truth.

THE WHITE STOAT

DAYTIME planned, all the house in flower,
Sheep and horses by the garden wall,
Model tractor in a valley hand,
This farm could be a toy, harmless and serene;

But the grey busy doves give it away,
Hard ringed eyes, birds of Aphrodite,
And the yowling tomcat out in the dark—
Under the moon another dispensation,

Hollow night, Astarte and the frozen stars,
Mice taken by the arrow-silent owl,
Fingers to claw, grudges and spite to bear,
And a white stoat arched in the bow of hate.

OPERATION OF MEMORY

How well I remember the rock basin
As warm as two cupped hands, the spray
And the waterfall on to a brown stone
When they came to take me away,
Ignoring my young brother,
Putting a hand on my shoulder,
Taking me to the waiting car,
The white corridors and ether—

The cupped hands of the rock brimming
A lip of flame in the small pool
And the rainbow second singing
To the cool talk of the waterfall;
I might have missed the drowned head
Of the rippling stone,
Might never have noticed
The reddening afternoon
If they had not come to take me away,
The sense of dread sharpening the eye.

"SERVYN", 4/5/78

THE word into the deed, rotten forests rise again,
Petroleum into plastic; and art, and hardware,
All at the service of a game, for gain,
They formed her in her cradle in the Yard,

Yet, as the prow thrust out to meat the day
Down to the sea on a trailer, bone-clean,
She did not wear the look of a toy—
She came out like a sword drawn from the stone.

PICTURE

MOUNTAINS shaped like a child's drawing
Of mountains; thunder across the sea
Over which a fluky wind sent warning.

Under a fist of sulky
Cloud like a purple
Catalyst, suddenly
Fighting for survival;

Gunwale dipping to the enemy,
Jibsheet a bar of iron,
The spray blinding—

A small boat alone on the horizon,
Just like a child's drawing.

A LOW PROFILE

LIFE is the slime at the meeting of land and sea;
Ancient sea-coasts long dry are betrayed
By the fossil line of the blue-green algae;
At the same rate as winter, rain, and flood,
Periwinkles wear away the rocks, slow filing,
Teeth on a ribbon the substance of insects' wings,
Persistent, proof against gales, a low profile;
The headland-breaking roller flings
Against the mussel beds a million tons
Green, dead weight and the wild smother
Where the immense backwash foams down—
They offer only silken threads for anchor—

Mussels, micro-plants, predatory whelks outlive
God's anger and the tides; we notice how
Such weakly anchored natures can survive
Knowledge of politics, philosophy, Dachau.

JUDGEMENT

The blade-keen rush in the surf of the longboat landing
Carried a horror, a greedy, bloody aggression;
The gilded oaken prisons of Nelson's commanding
Were slave-ships extending oppression;
Like enough, posterity will find your boats beautiful,
But will turn the eye of judgement on you;
It is one thing to see the grace of the flying hull,
Quite another to pardon the crew.

SIGNAL

PRIMARY colours for single-letter signals
Pennants against a nursery sky,
The Flag Alphabet has a toyshop appeal
But no signals are simple—take the I,
A yellow square, a black ball at the centre,
A baleful, dominant, accusing eye;
There is more to me than guilt, but when I enter
My own identity I must start with I—
On the deepest level I—
Incommunicable and as sealed as O.

GIANT SWING

As one professional gymnast, he was two:
Above the waist, a giant-killer that threw
Loops over gravity with grace; below,
A little twinkling servant in tight trews.
He was precise within his chosen field,
Violence into art, he loved the discipline,
Parallel bars to fence him from the world:
And made me stay, in Nineteen Thirty-Nine
When I said I could not pay the fee,
Answered, "Please come, all your friends here are mine—
You haven't learned the Giant Swing, you see—
If you stop training now you'll fall behind."
The words exactly suitable to Herman
Set up their own Giant Swing in the mind:
Kind, mild, and german.

TO GET READY FOR A JOURNEY

To get ready for a journey, set out for the desert,
New ventures, the mountain range, the plain
Brought me to boating and the renewed start,
Every day full of hope again—

Not to deny disease, and war, and crime,
Nor to pretend there is no such thing
As unhappiness, poverty, time,
But to let the golden figurehead sing!

It's certain we build our craft in fear and failure,
All hulls whatever go down to final ruin
Gilded like the Fighting Temeraire
It may be in splendour: it is disintegration.

Shall we set out, then, one more time?
Let us not give up the morning for his sake
Though Death be felt as the pull of the tidal streams
Unmaking as they make.

THE COAST

It is a coast for shipwreck,
Rocky, inhospitable, cliff-bound,
Battered by the full mature decision,
The headland-breaking waves of the Pacific;
There are no houses, only a colony
Of mutton-birds on a tower of black stone,
And in the ocean, seals and tiger-sharks.

A three-master came ashore in Cathedral Bay,
The survivors died of exposure on the beach,
Unable to climb the walls. Their neglected graves
Have long been lost and forgotten. Nowadays
There are steps cut in the stone, but nobody swims there.

From the main inland road, every track
Bears a skull-and-crossbones warning,
With the words, "Lonely road, no water."

Ship's crews, visiting the tall island,
Would slaughter barrels of mutton-birds,
A leathery, foul meat, and sail away.

The Aurora Australis, ice-blink of the grave
Flickers, riding the distant horizon.

The sound of the sea is imperious,
Such a boom when the long rollers hit,
White spray climbing a hundred feet—
Reminds me I am foreign to it all,
Sea birds, dark fish, long cliffs
And the wet red forest of the seaweed.

Occasionally a lone sail
Still stands inshore, a shark hunter
Working for liver-oil.

The atmosphere is turbulent and bitter,
Austere and desolate, its quality
Defying me, as night after night
I dream I hear the breakers on the rocks.

THE GAOLER

(Caelum, non animum, mutant
Qui trans mare currunt.
Horace.)

On the sea, first of all the lilting
Thought of the town left behind me,
The documents, the conflicting
Claims for attention—
naturally
slowly
Sails adopted the harmony
Of gulls to the gale, of seals to the swirl,
And sure as grey dawn the cacophony
Died away—
silence began to swell
Beyond creak and sigh and engine
Over the labouring sea-shaped hull
Until it became as noise had been,
The gaoler inside my sky-deep skull
Who cursed the rigging, longed for the shore,
Spliced the hours into a noose
Around the neck of the albatross
That screamed to be free, as it had screamed before.

TO IMPOSE A SEA CHANGE

When you ask, "What am I doing here?"
The wind rising again,
After you thought the gale blown out—
The sail to be changed down,
Ropes wild as snakes, spitfire
Flogging like a fiend,
Deck rolling out of control,
Shins barked, knuckles skinned,
Spray like gravel in your face,
Eyes blind with salt,
Ears full of the storm voice,
No dry clothes, no heat—

It answers, "The animals
Are now let out of the cage,
This place for you is natural,
The question is survival, and
You must learn the language."

Though not in words: the gale
Is its own form, contains
Itself, the centre of will;
The foam hard driven
Along the dancing hills
Rising and falling, pistons
In walls of a pewter hell,
All drift, swing, motion
Lives and dies by law,
And the calms and the currents
Are like your presence there—

Made whole, free in restraint,
And being the answer.

WHAT GROTESQUE VERSION

We people the water with our fantasies,
Memories of what we have done and what we have read,
History, regattas, imagined Argosies,
And our inventions of the dead.
No matter who they were, our fondest loves,
They were alone, as we under these skies;
We must create them from the material we have,
Our imagination happy with its lies.
And when we have gone, and others refuse to guess
What we were, having their own joys and sorrows,
What grotesque version of our loneliness
Will skim the bay with the delicate sea-swallows.

GONE AWAY

THE cold air crystal clear like a bell
Ringing the risen morning in the Bay,
Light gilds the moment, a fine spell
Spangles the seaway.
In praise of escapist thoughts, a gentle wind
Draws white clouds against a limpid sky,
And the quay murmurs of little waves to a mind
That has turned away,
Slipped off, into the amber light of the past,
Into the old ways of the holiday
Held in a world that had been made to stay,
A world built by nostalgia out of care,
That never was, wish for it though we may;
Where, in the singing at the end of the year,
Fear's cold went away.

WAKE

The wake, like a woman's photograph;
For an instant the fluid forms display
The individual impressed upon the ocean,
Time and space and the loved one on her way.

WHALES

THEY haunt me in the city of the night
        Ridiculous, agile as clouds,
        Stronger than storms.
When we saw them they were otherwise engaged,
        And their puffing into the air
        Was like cattle.
They were bourgeois and slick and wallowing
        In family life, resting.
        We sailed away very quietly.
I have seen hills that were more like Leviathan.
        They disappointed our expectations,
        Leaving nothing when they sounded

But the dream of weightless irresistible forms
Driving down into the grave of the dark.

AFTER

Over this sea there are no more fishing boats,
Just the desolate wind darkening the water,
The blast of the sun fire, and the surf
Working the shingle;
Over the horizon, not one sailing boat
Nor the boxlike superstructure of the liners,
Just dawn seeping in at the broken roof,
And Sirius, and the white thistle.

LIMITS OF KNOWLEDGE

We can make up stories about it
Embroider metaphors
Draw legitimate inference from it
Of effect and cause

The candle flame in the quiet room
The shadows dancing
And the moth flying out of the gloom
To a ritual burning

Apart from the phenomenon of fire
And the art of flight
Tossed on fluttering wings of straw
There is the insect,

The feathery antennae set to play
That other language
The curled tongue ready to relay
A flower's message

That being unaware of menace
Riding its nerves
Feeling the need for the furnace
Part of its life

That ends in a flop and a snuff
A pathetic fizz—
The happening is strange enough
But the best of it is

Those multiple eyes contain
The insect glow.
What the moth finds in the flame
We can never know.

SUNKEN CHURCH, CITTADUCALE

You climb down, having parked the car;
Under the eaves you look into the nave,
A sounding hollow, treetop deep, bizarre,
Less like a Cathedral than a cave,
Below you, echoing bat country;
Then there are bushes—you push down
To find the stone facade a tipsy sentry
Dreaming over a diamond stream that drowns
The doorstep and the floor in purity,
In waterweeds and tadpoles, fish and flies—
Its architecture lacks all clarity,
A style declining flight and enterprise,
But now, among the trees, the walls leaning,
Without a roof, unsafe, quiet,
It calls for nightingales and evening
And someone standing alone to watch the light.

THE CIRCLE CLOSES

The circle closes on the driven game,
At first it is so wide they do not know
They go toward the centre just the same.
The weeks have gone by since the horsemen came,
The grazing animals are moving slow,
The circle closes on the driven game,
The tiger feeds, the spotted deer are tame,
Nature has only flying fear to show
They go toward the centre just the same.
Until the very end they have no claim,
Beasts to the slaughter, herded in a row,
The circle closes on the driven game,
But when they die, their bodies leave the blame
Square on the shoulders of both high and low,
Who go toward the centre just the same.
The vultures circle in, spreading the fame;
The men are left to one another now;
The circle closes on the driven game,
They go toward the centre just the same.

HADRIAN'S VILLA

(For Peter Finch)

THICK weeds on a bare skyline,
A fat and disgruntled guardian,
Green lizards flick, the rebuilt
Pool stares flatly at the brick wall,
It is all so hot and the thorns
Crackle.
        But below the hill
In the overgrown theatre
As you recited his dying verse
Sheep, like souls, flowed in to crop the grass.

DANCING

NOT by chance the walls and muscles of the heart
Curve to the windings of the deep-sea shell,
The blood forms the holes where the weed waves
To the beat of the ocean felt in the pulse of the swell,
And the hunting sharks swim out of the warm dark caves
Following the blood trail—endlessly they range
Further and faster, yet they are animals
Borne up by that element, their nature strange
To the wide-faring piracy of the screaming gulls.

Reason relies on the muscles of the heart
To send the breakers crashing in the gales
And support the hunters in their endless dance
Following, racing along the ribbon trails,
The free brain's dance within the cells of chance,
Free inside the element under the calls
Of the blood trail and the shape of the seven seas—
Angelic measure of freewheeling gulls—
The steps are like the dance of the honey-bees—

The wind that bends the muscles of the heart
Sends the bees to the honey, and the wondering sharks
Knifing into the darkly foreign seas—
The dancers weave free in the city parks
Deserving of pity in their necessity,
Following their instinct down the canyon streets,
Acting as if their movements were their own,
Sheltering from the rain in the bee-soft sheets,
And seeing the gulls ride inland on the storm.

HEARD, SHARED AND REMEMBERED

CONTEMPLATION gives the machine a gender;
The steady creation of reality strives
To marry what we see to what lies under;
Without the living, loving cannot thrive.

She rises to the live swell like a dream,
In us and of us and solid on the wave
And over the miles she dances to a theme
Heard, shared and remembered.

We are sharing it with water, and with the strong
Seagoing structure that engineering gave,
But full and fulfilling, it is the Siren Song—
Too late for warning now—she is alive.

BLIND CHESS

THE squid behind his cloud of ink,
The actor in his tragic part,
The Council Chairman, make you think
How much is there, how much is art.

We had to make the God we made
Omniscient, and omnipotent,
Able to pierce the inky shade
To see which way the heart was bent.

But now that we have lost His glance,
We are abandoned to Blind Chess,
A game that gives us all a chance—
We can't see them, they can't see us.

FOCUS

TAKE a new boat flying downwind, sails full,
A steady response to the tiller's tension,
The rush of the surfing line of the hull
In the flurry of action;
Silence below, everything stowed,
The spread of the light red spi in the sun,
The starcut white, the green luff bowed,
Empty horizon, she dances alone;
Bright spray blown off blue wave walls,
The spirit lifting as she surges after
The seas as they run and rise and fall,
And the wheeling gulls, and laughter:

But a little time and a short way,
The hull grows old, the ensign frays in the wind—
Remember the sway of the sail on the sky of that day,
Focus the mind.

THE FACTS

THE facts are bare, merely a list of parts,
Mast boom sail pair of winches samson post;
Lovely sound hull free from injury or marks,
Engine a real beauty, more cared-for than most;
To be washed, painted, repaired for a wage,
Sold Bought Resold till old, for a percentage.

We take the facts and with them generate
A face, a welcome out of our own hearts;
Love itself is born of gazing, we create
Something in which we merely play a part—
A servitude, a dreaming that compiles
The clear days,
        and the soft air,
                and the fortunate isles.

SENSE

DAWN with a lunar light,
        Sea and sky silent,
High tide, sand white,
        The harpooner patient—
Seaweed waves aside
        From knife-handed crabs,
Betrays where fish hide
        And the spearman stabs
To disturb the shark form
        Of the boat's dark shade
As the surface is torn
        By the splash that's made.

No word. Near the red rocks
        In the distance, loud,
A sea-eagle shivers and shocks
        The silence, his proud
Stooping explodes in spray,
        Then the hushed air closes—
The leopard eyes of a great ray
        Appear—the spear lunges.
It fights with a strong wing
        And a devil's face,
Jabbing its long sting
        With terrible force,
Tosses the sea white,
        Magnificent, plumed
With spray, its last fight
        Foreseen, foredoomed
By the fine harpoon
        That hoists its prey
And dumps it down
        On the deck to die.

As it arches and flops
    Its torn agony
From its pale belly pops
    A newborn stingray—
The austerity of day recedes,
    We stoop with care,
Smile, give him the sea he needs,
    Laugh at him there,
A perfect small being
    Diving through the clear tide
Of all that we were seeing
    To his future pride—

The sense of a design that has
    No sense in words,
And yet the pattern possesses
    The flight of birds
And the fall of the small ray
    Wavering to confirm
Its shadow's light play
    On the sandbar form.

IN THE TELESCOPE OF THE SEXTANT

In the telescope of the Sextant you hope to see
The fixed lights ready—the horizon mirror
Bring them to heel, and on the scale of degree
You will turn the drum to adjust the vernier:

The sun becomes a bottle-green globe, sliding
About in one man's hand that can not control
The horizon riding up and down and reading
Whatever he makes of it, and never still,

The planets shiver because we are of dust,
The stars fly out of the mirror's universe,
And what they do, they do because they must;
We measure them at last, commanding space,

But when we put the nautical Tables down
The ancient Gods come out of the preterite—
Aphrodite rises above the dawn,
And Mars, one small red eye on the satellites.

LES MOINES

For an object whose height is known in advance
Take a Sextant angle, measuring,
Enter the Table and read off the distance—
But in the mist we went by reckoning.

I knew the rotten tooth, half eaten away,
The tower called Le Prêtre and the mile of reef
Known as les moines, and sailing confidently
Set a course to pass between rock and cliff;

In cold grey air the oily swell was clear
And suddenly boiled a swirl, right by the lee,
Where a granite hand reached near—
We were off, only by the scend of the sea—

Dead reckoning and in error—almost
Taken among the adamantine nuns
Like Heretics, to be broken
On the sunken reef, and lost.

NAVIGATION

THE precise light of the stars
Is not impersonal,
Only to us it seems so, because
We look too far for the nature of our eyes.

When we think of ultimate things
There is in the brain that brilliance
Of a pattern wheeling and freezing
Around a cardinal direction—

So we are sometimes driven
To forget they have a purpose
When applied to this familiar hive,
This satellite of ours;

They light us home,
Measure the year, and teach
How terrestrial the mind's grasp
Compared to the glory of its reach.

THE FIRST MORNING

GULLS, cold air, morning
Created for the first time
Innocent of meaning
Without man, word, system—

I saw an albatross trail his wing
Down waves as great as this whole port,
High as houses, walled with rain,
The Antarctic sky storm-shot—

Nets, iridescent oily scum, hulls
Weaving and burning for the first morning,
The new day and the gulls new
Until words come to blur the sign;

All there, the prehistoric light
And again, the individual
New and unique, conjured from the night
To find the words worn thin and dull—

I saw the silver belly of a dolphin
Flash in the spray,
Cross the bows and sound
Down and away;
Waves ran on and remained,
The hull heeled over to the wind,
Down beyond words it sounded,
A fountain contained in the mind—

The gentle images sing, the gulls
Fulfil the air, their wings reveal
How nearly the individual
Contains the spell,

Signs spelling the wordless fountain
Music ordering forms of light
Around the talisman
Of things united.

The power in the sound
Transcends the port,
Wave and ocean, wing and wind
In the tension of art;
Made new again
The cliché of dust
Spells out the fountain,
Writes albatross,
The waves cry summertime Venus,
Words quicken and combine,
Transition, synthesis:
Singing a rainbow from yesterday's bones.

INLAND AT LAST

LIKE a domestic animal, riding the tide
After her distance run, the sailing done,
Gently snubbing the mooring where she is tied,
At rest from the sun,

I can see her leaving the working sea of the coast,
Leaving the fleet, and the lights, and the noise of the band,
Setting out quietly, not the expected way,
But alone, inland;

Heading in darkness over the sacred stones,
Over the fertile heartland to her fate
In the mirror pool of silence, among the bones
Where the furies wait;

Fading between the graves and the ancient trees,
Following the course others have made before,
Fully laden, one of the Argosies
To be seen no more;

Sinking past clouds where the scudding moonbeams show
The waves of resonance drowning out the mast,
The wreck calling the sailor where he must go,
Inland at last.

THE VISITORS

In overfalls of yelling Autumn gales
We still find echoes of the Summer's thrill,
And the wild flurry on the grey sea-walls
Recalls the deck awash, the sea-boots full;
When shivering down the coast the lightest wind
Sends fish-scales quivering over the calm surface
They waken in the mind the slamming, blind
Boredom of the sails' limp helplessness—
Did Ulysses never grow old and lose the chance
Of the moment in its generous vitality?
Is it true, then, we must lose our resonance,
Looking like visitors at a remembered sea?
Do they miss it, when it finally dies away
Leaving no wake in time as the hull no furrow,
The whisper that gives depth to the sailing day,
The sea around us, promising tomorrow?

THE OPTIMISTS

In the morning we can say
"It is not too late,
The faith and values we surrender today
Are turned by Time into a sort of hate,
But from them the vines of the new planting grow"—
We must think so. But evening falls,
The tide is on the ebb, vitality low,
And from nightmare the vengeance calls—

In the morning we can say "It is not too late,
Perhaps it won't happen, the Revelation;
The figures of the Dream of John are out of date,
We no longer believe in a God of Damnation,
You cannot terrorise us in that way."
As we see the coloured sails, the race begun,
Optimists in line to tack across the bay,
A mushroom cloud passes over the sun.

BY THE PLOUGH

ALDEBARAN, Sirius, Al Na'ir—
Call them out to serve and magically
On a clear night, steering by the stars
There is no loneliness on the empty sea;
The constellations are a false display
And yet their names can set the mind alight
Remembering the Astronomers, and they
Had names to give a reverence to the night;
They silver the Admiralty of sailing men
Like moons glittering upon us here, as bright
As one thought of Titania and Oberon,
Those twin satellites—
No longer empty ocean, lonely hours,
The names are beacon towers to guide us now,
The seas of history are white with fires
And we are driving steady by the Plough.

GONE

THEY are motoring down the canal and past the moorings
Strong figures in sunlight moving about on board
And they wave, making her ready for the crossing,
In a hurry to get off, on their way abroad.
Further out, they turn to the wind to begin,
The white wings flutter and ruffle and rise to hover
For the swerve and swoop when they are sheeted in
And are set to draw, heeling her over.
Steady as she goes, she goes with a bone in her teeth
Becoming faint with the haze of the summer season,
Far off she seems as unmoving as the sea underneath
Until she is fading away on a dim horizon.
The heart aches, seeing them hull-down from the shore,
With something like the regret for things not done,
Journeys not to be made now, any more,
All left too late and the opportunity gone.

SUMMER CALM

SKY a grey pearl, and on it one pink planet
That hangs above a sea dove-grey over the deep,
Pale smoke swells in the bay, where a little fleet
Among seagulls floating folded, lines the shore of sleep;
Its anchor-lights are planets half afloat
That seep out of a sea cool, sweet, serene;
The last windsurfer drifts toward his boat,
The children and the singing birds pipe down;
When the dark rises and the summer haze,
The yachts at anchor, dinghies, rocks and pool,
The old Fort and the sky all huddle close,
The shell of sleep itself, mother-of-pearl.

STILL NIGHT

THE cold sea no longer seems normal,
It is dusted with gold over its quiet surface,
Shadow from shadow divided by a veil,
The faintest trace.
Our wake is a nebula, a whirling mane
And where we pass, the bow wave burning out,
Plankton swirling like the fires of pale suns
Each one turning dark satellites about.

A change of temperature has thrown a gauze,
A ribbon of pale haze along the horizon,
And under that, there seem to be fireflies—
The starblink is jewelling the ocean—

Beyond number, eyes beyond time, they bathe,
Worlds cooling in our finite pool of sight.
Our navigation lights burn on a little hearth,
Sky underneath us, and we are a hole in the night.

HAUNTED BY THE SEA

EVERY City casts a glow
Fungus-rotten in the dark,
The steady beat of traffic comes in waves—
A twisted tree grows
From black fossils of the teeth of sharks,
Dunes swallow the desert graves—
In rocks above the snowline
Prints of the shells of Ammonites,
The walls twist in mechanically—
No escape, confined
Within these limits,
Haunted by the sea.

IN KIT FORM

DRESSING mahogany that cuts like bread
And smells to a sensual man like a sacrament,
Pressing sheets of marine ply into the red
Dried blood of the glue in a mould so exactly bent,
Driving a thousand golden screws of brass,
Tightening the silver bolts of stainless steel,
Painting the magic resin into the glass,
Sanding the stucco on the cast iron keel;
Blessing with varnish the flesh of wooden cleats,
Getting the waterline painted where she floats—
The Craft of boatbuilding somewhere in all this meets
The crafty delight of mucking about in boats.

STRETTO DI PIOMBINO

It is a terrible thing to sail down through the Strait
On a perfect afternoon in Spring,
The waves beginning to show their crests in white,
The Maestraletto blowing, the sea rising,
The boat going as though she were on show,
Taking the waves like surf, and the underlying
Joy of home-waters, and not far to go,
And that sad, unforgettable note of the gulls crying:

They will tear at your hearts, you poor fools,
When the time shall come that you are done sailing;
Memories with the hard, sharp eyes of gulls
Wheeling and calling.

WINTER IN TOWN

CALLING up in the mind, beyond any anxiety,
The white hull heeling at the moment she feels the wind,
In an ideal bay under a cloudless sky,
Full of that light reflected blinding from the sand:
Any small detail—the tiller varnished like glass—
The feel of the smooth pull as she begins to run,
Docile to the hand: an intense happiness
Begins to burn with the vibration of the sun,
And out of consciousness I am relaxing into light,
There is no more boundary to any part of the day;
The wind and the sand and that unbearable white
Have filled the sails of a great ship, standing away.

ST. FLORENT, CORSICA

A perfect setting for the holiday scene,
Cafés, flowering umbrellas, the Harbour,
Crowds of us soaking up with summer sun
Some hours of meaning to the months of labour.
Attention follows the swifts, pauses to linger
On houses leaning together, gathered to
The grey Church spire, a meaningful finger
Pointing to layers of nothing coloured blue;
Beyond the masts and rigging, beyond the bay,
The mountains line the background with their bones,
And along them, all day long, the colours play
Their silent music of evolution;
Outside the human dimension, abstract colonies
Of colour rise out of the mountain chain,
The rocks dreaming their rose and purple dyes.

CONQUEST

THE crew is one macroscopic fact
With an élite cell curbing it, but free
Within limits set by ambition, tact,
Solidarity, rules, the working of the sea;
The brain is another: get near to a thought,
Approach the nervous component of a cell,
It will fake dead, or repelled, or different;
We need a Theory of Systems for it all,
For History, for the Skull—suddenly I see
A new Henry the Navigator, drawing charts,
Projecting voyages of discovery,
The Ocean of Ideas, Indies of Art;
Nations and notions mapped
Towards, who knows,
The feathered warriors trapped,
The Conquest of what golden Mexicos.

THE WANDERER

He did not like what this life has to offer;
He wanted what he wanted. Movement stilled
The pain that stillness always made him suffer.
Fishing off Land's End one night he was killed.
Wandering was ever his true fancy;
He has lost the being lost since he has died,
And staying in his proper buoyancy
He does not swing with, he becomes the tide.

YOU GO HE

THREE peaks, then a low-lying promontory,
Seen through dawn mist, the sun on my back—
Not unlike Montecristo, with rocks from my history—
And the sea turbulent, and the sky black:
Always to be arriving would discourage Reason
Who must push the visit to its one true end;
First, the scent of the herbs warmed on the stones,
Then the entrance, with its awkward bend;
All proceeds in order to the One-Two-Three,
From the Port, to the mooring, to the fairlead, to the deck,
From the hatchway, to the cabin, to the "You Go He",
But that is not the end, and it is not luck.
The game goes on, past the power to be clear,
From the He, to the rib-cage, to the heart pumping blind,
To the caves, to the darkness, to the shapes in the air
That are shadows cast by light, that dawns to find
In a turbulent sea, three peaks of an Island.

WINTER FOR QUIET

Gulls to the garbage tip and to follow the plough,
Sun to the filth of driving clouds and wrack,
What we have is a winter theorem now,
In grey and black.
Now life is running down, and the result
Of rising air and rapidly falling pressure
Is the bare, inevitable tumult
Of atmosphere.
As it moves, it drives the water along
In wave trains that reflect geography,
That illustrate how tall wet cliffs are strong
In their geology.
Like a trigger release, like two plus two makes four,
What is prepared out there, punctually arrives;
The windows stream, the storm slams shut the door
Like a shot ending lives.
If only engine earth could stay like this,
Natural forces following simple laws,
Never a judgement, a misery or a bliss,
No truth, no flaws—
Spring for the sudden shooting hopes and fears,
Summer for the full political riot,
Autumn for funerals and, no-one to hear,
Winter for quiet—
But as sure as war and hemlock, the year will turn,
Spring will be caught out one fine day in green
And the crop of delusions, deceptions, dreams will return
With the sailing machines.

HOLIDAY

THE praying trees can hardly breathe the shade,
Sky pale with heat, the traffic furnace roars,
Sea lies prostrate, an unconscious nude,
As the crowd appears.

Too many, and the beach becomes a war,
The water cannot cool them all at once,
The sea would steam; and every little Bar
Now harvests the chance.

An army of refugees from anxiety
Anxiously seeks the refuge offered them,
And tries to sink into a society
That despises them.

Time is in ambush, its revenge is sure,
A few more days, it all comes pressing in,
The movement underfoot that has no future,
The guilt felt as sin.

The feeling that the process has gone wrong,
That the powerful are powerless to save,
That they cannot offer comfort on the long
Retreat to the grave.

And near at hand the Marina shines like glass,
One sort of Good Life paid for and affected,
The lovely laughing fauna of the masts,
They look protected.

Penned up like well-fed cattle for the thieves,
They manage to forget the single vote;

The fact of being rich enough receives
More than just a boat.

The poor enough are like the sea, in that
They can be stirred up to destroy the wall,
But left alone the waves lie very flat,
When they move at all.

Far out to sea a sail shows like a hand;
One likes to think that he has found the track
To the brotherhood of never-never land,
And will not come back.

BUT—

THERE is so little to show how swiftly the years have gone.

The ebb leaves behind on the sand a wide
Pattern of ribs, and it cannot be denied
How the beach is desolate down to the sea
That was once alive, pounded by the spring tide,
And becomes the pain of this desert before me.

The white on the wave is also the wind
On the sand, and the ribs are gone,
Are blown quite away; yet the shore
Will again be pounded by the flow into bone,
And the pattern will be the same as before—

But where a new-won inlet bears witness my time is done.

KNOWLEDGE

KNOWLEDGE hangs a hawk shade
Over the sunny playground
Cannot pretend it was not done,
The brains dashed out, the ovens—

Clear voices ring in the glade
Like a trumpet call,
Lower down the overgrown orchard
Speaks of the worm-eaten windfall,
In such long grass we lay together
And knew nothing at all.

MOORING FLOWERS

THE wide twin-screw diesel luxury cruisers
Ablaze with reflected expense, flourish a vice:
They must unfurl gladioli, the mooring flowers,
To display their space.

In a line of these fine yachts, fender to fender,
One exhibited more power and polish than grace,
And as the lights came on, we gathered to stare
In respectful silence:

There to be seen behind panes of tinted glass
Were two vases of mooring flowers, a tiger-lily,
A cactus in a ceramic bowl and, last,
A tiny model sailing-ship, to remind us of the sea.

CRUISING IN AUTUMN

YOUNG cries in October mist, echoing down the quay,
It is still high summer for them, and the hour of roses;
They can go on ignoring the face of *memento mori*
Till the smile closes.
Dogma and faith do not make walls of oak,
Men will be what they are; the fool, the fool;
Nothing can save the servant from the yoke;
The ruler will rule.
Cruising in Autumn, in between the gales,
We know the Spring comes, but the boat knows age,
Time that puts hour on hour till the structure fails,
Not worth the salvage;
The petal of any flower that must end forever,
But for a moment the fragrance of summer is there again
Like an old fever.

AFTERWORD

A number of years ago, in Rome, I was standing at one end of the bar in Rosati's with a couple of artist friends. Well into the evening I announced in a loud and not entirely sober voice that, "the two greatest novelists who ever lived were Leo Tolstoy and P.G. Wodehouse." On hearing this pronouncement, a burly, handsome dark-haired man came barrelling towards me from the opposite side of the room and shook my hands. This dynamic and enthusiastic being was B.R. Whiting, who insisted that we accompany him and his wife to their apartment in Trastevere. There, with a flourish, he showed us quite the most impressive collection of the works of Wodehouse in several languages, that I've ever seen. Our mutual love of the works of the Master turned out to be only one bond between us: poetry was another, as were the glorious paintings of his wife, Lorri. But though we talked so intensely of poetry and art, with an odd reticence in so ebullient a man, Bertie Whiting never showed me poems of his own. Only now that he is gone are we able to fully share that bond between us. How I would have loved to have said, "Bertie, your poems are so wonderfully felt, so beautifully made! And like Lorri's painting, they are so full of the sea, of wind and sails . . . Best of all is your clear-sighted unflinching take on what life is all about." And so much more . . .

Ours was a friendship nourished by very few occasions. But it survived the years when we did not meet, as these poems survive time—and the man and the poems together live beyond his death.

—Carolyn Kizer

In the Mountains, 1981

BIOGRAPHICAL NOTE

B.R. Whiting was born in Melbourne, Australia in 1923. He died in Rome in 1989. He was educated at Geelong Grammar, Melbourne. He served in the Australian Army and held all ranks to Captain, Paratroops. Enjoying the end of British Raj as A.D.C. to Governor of Bengal, he went from those palaces to beekeeping in a tent in the Australian Desert. He has been a journalist, script writer, playwright, carpenter, and researcher. He was married to the painter Lorri and settled in Rome in 1955.